OMAD COOKBOOK

MAIN COURSE - 60+ Easy to prepare at home recipes for a balanced and healthy diet

TABLE OF CONTENTS

BREAKFAST 5
BLUEBERRY PANCAKES 5
NECTARINE PANCAKES 6
BANANA PANCAKES 7
ONION PANCAKES 8
PANCAKES 9
MANDARIN MUFFINS 10
BANANA MUFFINS 11
POMEGRANATE MUFFINS 12
STRAWBERRY MUFFINS 13
PLUMS MUFFINS 14
MUFFINS 15
POTATO OMELETTE 16
ZUCCHINI OMELETTE 17
BASIL OMELETTE 18
MUSHROOM OMELETTE 19
PUMPKIN OMELETTE 20
BLUEBERRIES OATMEAL 21
CHIA PUDDING 22
BREAKFAST CASSEROLE 23
BLUEBERRY BALLS 24
ZUCCHINI BREAD 25
LUNCH 27
TOMATO FRITATTA 27
YAM ROOT FRITATTA 28
WATERCRESS FRITATTA 29
ZUCCHINI FRITATTA 30

BROCCOLI FRITATTA	31
MOZZARELLA STUFFED CHICKEN BREAST	32
MACARONI AND CHEESE	33
BUTTERNUT SQUASH BISQUE	34
GARLIC CHICKEN	35
PASTA WITH CREAM SAUCE	36
ROASTED SALAD	37
PUMPKIN SALAD	38
DUCK SALAD	39
BRUSSELS SPROUT SALAD	40
ANTI-INFLAMMATORY SALAD	41
RED CHICORY SALAD	42
FENNEL SALAD	43
GIGNER CILANTRO SALAD	44
DINNER	45
CHEESE MACARONI	45
POTATO CASSEROLE	46
CHEESE STUFFED SHELLS	47
POTATO SOUP	48
CHICKEN ALFREDO	50
BUTTERNUT SQUASH PIZZA	52
PENNE WITH ASPARAGUS	53
NOODLE SOUP	54
TOMATO WRAP	56
THYME COD	57
VEGGIE STIR-FRY	58
SMOOTHIES	59
PROBIOTIC SMOOTHIE	59

ENERGY BOOSTING SMOOTHIE	60
BLUEBERRY SMOOTHIE	61
RED CAPSICUM JUICE	62
GREEN SMOOTHIE	63
RASPBERRY MOJITO FRAPPE	64
MANGO SMOOTHIE	65
PINEAPPLE SMOOTHIE	66
BLUEBERRIES SMOOTHIE	67
PEANUT BUTTER & BANANA SMOOTHIE	68
GROOVY SMOOTHIE	69

Copyright 2020 by Sussane Davis - All rights reserved.

This document is geared towards providing exact and reliable information in regards to the topic and issue covered. The publication is sold with the idea that the publisher is not required to render accounting, officially permitted, or otherwise, qualified services. If advice is necessary, legal or professional, a practiced individual in the profession should be ordered.

- From a Declaration of Principles which was accepted and approved equally by a Committee of the American Bar Association and a Committee of Publishers and Associations.

In no way is it legal to reproduce, duplicate, or transmit any part of this document in either electronic means or in printed format. Recording of this publication is strictly prohibited and any storage of this document is not allowed unless with written permission from the publisher. All rights reserved.

The information provided herein is stated to be truthful and consistent, in that any liability, in terms of inattention or otherwise, by any usage or abuse of any policies, processes, or directions contained within is the solitary and utter responsibility of the recipient reader. Under no circumstances will any legal responsibility or blame be held against the publisher for any reparation, damages, or monetary loss due to the information herein, either directly or indirectly.

Respective authors own all copyrights not held by the publisher.

The information herein is offered for informational purposes solely, and is universal as so. The presentation of the information is without contract or any type of guarantee assurance.

The trademarks that are used are without any consent, and the publication of the trademark is without permission or backing by the trademark owner. All trademarks and brands within this book are for clarifying purposes only and are the owned by the owners themselves, not affiliated with this document.

Introduction

OMAD recipes for personal enjoyment but also for family enjoyment. You will love them for sure for how easy it is to prepare them.

BREAKFAST

BLUEBERRY PANCAKES

Serves: **4**

Prep Time: **10** Minutes

Cook Time: **20** Minutes

Total Time: **30** Minutes

INGREDIENTS

- 1 cup whole wheat flour
- ¼ tsp baking soda
- ¼ tsp baking powder
- 1 cup blueberries
- 2 eggs
- 1 cup milk

DIRECTIONS

1. In a bowl combine all ingredients together and mix well
2. In a skillet heat olive oil
3. Pour ¼ of the batter and cook each pancake for 1-2 minutes per side
4. When ready remove from heat and serve

NECTARINE PANCAKES

Serves: **4**

Prep Time: **10** Minutes

Cook Time: **30** Minutes

Total Time: **40** Minutes

INGREDIENTS

- 1 cup whole wheat flour
- ¼ tsp baking soda
- ¼ tsp baking powder
- 1 cup nectarine
- 2 eggs
- 1 cup milk

DIRECTIONS

1. In a bowl combine all ingredients together and mix well
2. In a skillet heat olive oil
3. Pour ¼ of the batter and cook each pancake for 1-2 minutes per side
4. When ready remove from heat and serve

BANANA PANCAKES

Serves: *4*
Prep Time: *10* Minutes

Cook Time: *20* Minutes

Total Time: *30* Minutes

INGREDIENTS

- 1 cup whole wheat flour
- ¼ tsp baking soda
- ¼ tsp baking powder
- 1 cup mashed banana
- 2 eggs
- 1 cup milk

DIRECTIONS

1. In a bowl combine all ingredients together and mix well
2. In a skillet heat olive oil
3. Pour ¼ of the batter and cook each pancake for 1-2 minutes per side
4. When ready remove from heat and serve

ONION PANCAKES

Serves: *4*
Prep Time: *10* Minutes

Cook Time: **20**   Minutes

Total Time: **30**   Minutes

INGREDIENTS

- 1 cup whole wheat flour
- ¼ tsp baking soda
- ¼ tsp baking powder
- 1 cup onion
- 2 eggs
- 1 cup milk

DIRECTIONS

1. In a bowl combine all ingredients together and mix well
2. In a skillet heat olive oil
3. Pour ¼ of the batter and cook each pancake for 1-2 minutes per side
4. When ready remove from heat and serve

PANCAKES

Serves: **4**
Prep Time: **10**   Minutes

Cook Time: *30*   Minutes

Total Time: *40*   Minutes

INGREDIENTS

- 1 cup whole wheat flour
- ¼ tsp baking soda
- ¼ tsp baking powder
- 2 eggs
- 1 cup milk

DIRECTIONS

1. In a bowl combine all ingredients together and mix well
2. In a skillet heat olive oil
3. Pour ¼ of the batter and cook each pancake for 1-2 minutes per side
4. When ready remove from heat and serve

MANDARIN MUFFINS

Serves: *8-12*
Prep Time: *10*   Minutes

Cook Time: *20*   Minutes

Total Time: *30*   Minutes

INGREDIENTS

- 2 eggs
- 1 tablespoon olive oil
- 1 cup milk
- 2 cups whole wheat flour
- 1 tsp baking soda
- ¼ tsp baking soda
- 1 tsp ginger
- 1 cup mandarin
- ¼ cup molasses

DIRECTIONS

1. In a bowl combine all wet ingredients
2. In another bowl combine all dry ingredients
3. Combine wet and dry ingredients together
4. Pour mixture into 8-12 prepared muffin cups, fill 2/3 of the cups
5. Bake for 18-20 minutes at 375 F, when ready remove and serve

BANANA MUFFINS

Serves: *8-12*
Prep Time: *10*   Minutes
Cook Time: *20*   Minutes

Total Time: **30**   Minutes

INGREDIENTS

- 2 eggs
- 1 tablespoon olive oil
- 1 cup milk
- 2 cups whole wheat flour
- 1 tsp baking soda
- ¼ tsp baking soda
- 1 tsp cinnamon
- 1 cup mashed banana

DIRECTIONS

1. In a bowl combine all wet ingredients
2. In another bowl combine all dry ingredients
3. Combine wet and dry ingredients together
4. Fold in mashed banana and mix well
5. Pour mixture into 8-12 prepared muffin cups, fill 2/3 of the cups
6. Bake for 18-20 minutes at 375 F, when ready remove and serve

POMEGRANATE MUFFINS

Serves: **8-12**
Prep Time: **10**   Minutes
Cook Time: **20**   Minutes

Total Time: *30*   Minutes

INGREDIENTS

- 2 eggs
- 1 tablespoon olive oil
- 1 cup milk
- 2 cups whole wheat flour
- 1 tsp baking soda
- ¼ tsp baking soda
- 1 tsp cinnamon
- 1 cup pomegranate

DIRECTIONS

1. In a bowl combine all wet ingredients
2. In another bowl combine all dry ingredients
3. Combine wet and dry ingredients together
4. Pour mixture into 8-12 prepared muffin cups, fill 2/3 of the cups
5. Bake for 18-20 minutes at 375 F
6. When ready remove from the oven and serve

STRAWBERRY MUFFINS

Serves: *8-12*
Prep Time: *10*   Minutes
Cook Time: *20*   Minutes

Total Time: *30* Minutes

INGREDIENTS

- 2 eggs
- 1 tablespoon olive oil
- 1 cup milk
- 2 cups whole wheat flour
- 1 tsp baking soda
- ¼ tsp baking soda
- 1 tsp cinnamon
- 1 cup strawberries

DIRECTIONS

1. In a bowl combine all dry ingredients
2. In another bowl combine all dry ingredients
3. Combine wet and dry ingredients together
4. Fold in strawberries and mix well
5. Pour mixture into 8-12 prepared muffin cups, fill 2/3 of the cups
6. Bake for 18-20 minutes at 375 F, when ready remove and serve

PLUMS MUFFINS

Serves: *8-12*
Prep Time: *10* Minutes
Cook Time: *20* Minutes

Total Time: **30** Minutes

INGREDIENTS

- 2 eggs
- 1 tablespoon olive oil
- 1 cup milk
- 2 cups whole wheat flour
- 1 tsp baking soda
- ¼ tsp baking soda
- 1 tsp cinnamon
- 1 cup plums

DIRECTIONS

1. In a bowl combine all dry ingredients
2. In another bowl combine all dry ingredients
3. Combine wet and dry ingredients together
4. Pour mixture into 8-12 prepared muffin cups, fill 2/3 of the cups
5. Bake for 18-20 minutes at 375 F
6. When ready remove from the oven and serve

MUFFINS

Serves: **8-12**
Prep Time: **10** Minutes
Cook Time: **20** Minutes

Total Time: **30**   Minutes

INGREDIENTS

- 2 eggs
- 1 tablespoon olive oil
- 1 cup milk
- 2 cups whole wheat flour
- 1 tsp baking soda
- ¼ tsp baking soda
- 1 tsp cinnamon

DIRECTIONS

1. In a bowl combine all wet ingredients
2. In another bowl combine all dry ingredients
3. Combine wet and dry ingredients together
4. Pour mixture into 8-12 prepared muffin cups, fill 2/3 of the cups
5. Bake for 18-20 minutes at 375 F
6. When ready remove from the oven and serve

POTATO OMELETTE

Serves: **1**
Prep Time: **5**   Minutes
Cook Time: **10**   Minutes

Total Time: *15* Minutes

INGREDIENTS

- 2 eggs
- ¼ tsp salt
- ¼ tsp black pepper
- 1 tablespoon olive oil
- ¼ cup cheese
- ½ lb. sweet potato
- ¼ tsp basil

DIRECTIONS

1. In a bowl combine all ingredients together and mix well
2. In a skillet heat olive oil and pour the egg mixture
3. Cook for 1-2 minutes per side
4. When ready remove omelette from the skillet and serve

ZUCCHINI OMELETTE

Serves: *1*

Prep Time: *5* Minutes

Cook Time: *10* Minutes

Total Time: *15* Minutes

INGREDIENTS

- 2 eggs
- ¼ tsp salt
- ¼ tsp black pepper
- 1 tablespoon olive oil
- ¼ cup cheese
- ¼ tsp basil
- 1 cup zucchini

DIRECTIONS

1. In a bowl combine all ingredients together and mix well
2. In a skillet heat olive oil and pour the egg mixture
3. Cook for 1-2 minutes per side
4. When ready remove omelette from the skillet and serve

BASIL OMELETTE

Serves: 1
Prep Time: 5 Minutes
Cook Time: 10 Minutes
Total Time: 15 Minutes

INGREDIENTS

- 2 eggs
- ¼ tsp salt
- ¼ tsp black pepper
- 1 tablespoon olive oil
- ¼ cup cheese
- ¼ tsp basil
- 1 cup red onion

DIRECTIONS

1. In a bowl combine all ingredients together and mix well
2. In a skillet heat olive oil and pour the egg mixture
3. Cook for 1-2 minutes per side
4. When ready remove omelette from the skillet and serve

MUSHROOM OMELETTE

Serves: 1
Prep Time: 5 Minutes

Cook Time: 10 Minutes

Total Time: 15 Minutes

INGREDIENTS

- 2 eggs
- ¼ tsp salt
- ¼ tsp black pepper
- 1 tablespoon olive oil
- ¼ cup cheese
- ¼ tsp basil
- 1 cup mushrooms

DIRECTIONS

1. In a bowl combine all ingredients together and mix well
2. In a skillet heat olive oil and pour the egg mixture
3. Cook for 1-2 minutes per side
4. When ready remove omelette from the skillet and serve

PUMPKIN OMELETTE

Serves: *1*

Prep Time: *5* Minutes

Cook Time: *10* Minutes

Total Time: *15* Minutes

INGREDIENTS

- 2 eggs

- ¼ tsp salt
- ¼ tsp black pepper
- 1 tablespoon olive oil
- ¼ cup cheese
- ¼ tsp basil
- 1 cup pumpkin puree

DIRECTIONS

1. In a bowl combine all ingredients together and mix well
2. In a skillet heat olive oil and pour the egg mixture
3. Cook for 1-2 minutes per side
4. When ready remove omelette from the skillet and serve

BLUEBERRIES OATMEAL

Serves: 2
Prep Time: *10* Minutes

Cook Time: *8* Hours

Total Time: *8* Hours

INGREDIENTS

- 1/3 cup oats

- 1/3 cup blueberries
- 2 tbs maple syrup
- 1/3 cup coconut milk
- ½ tsp vanilla
- 1 banana
- 1 ½ tsp chia seeds

DIRECTIONS

1. Mix the oats and chia seeds together
2. Pour in the milk and top with blueberries and sliced banana
3. Refrigerate for at least 8 hours
4. Stir in the maple syrup and serve

CHIA PUDDING

Serves: 2
Prep Time: 5 Minutes
Cook Time: *10* Minutes
Total Time: *15* Minutes

INGREDIENTS

- 5 tbs chia seeds

- 1 ½ tbs vanilla
- 2 tbs maple syrup
- 2 ½ cup almond milk
- 1 ½ cup strawberries
- 1 beet

DIRECTIONS

1. Blend together the milk, strawberries, chopped beet, maple syrup, and vanilla
2. Pour into a cup and ad the chia
3. Stir every 5 minutes for 15 minutes
4. Refrigerate overnight
5. Serve topped with fruits

BREAKFAST CASSEROLE

Serves: 4

Prep Time: 10 Minutes

Cook Time: 35 Minutes

Total Time: 45 Minutes

INGREDIENTS

- 7 oz asparagus
- 3 tbs parsley

- 1 cup broccoli
- 1 zucchini
- 3 tbs oil
- 5 eggs
- Salt
- Pepper

DIRECTIONS

1. Cook the diced zucchini, asparagus and broccoli florets in heated oil for about 5 minutes
2. Season with salt and pepper and remove from heat
3. Whisk the eggs and season then add the parsley
4. Place the vegetables in a greased pan then pour the eggs over
5. Bake in the preheated oven for about 35 minutes at 350F

BLUEBERRY BALLS

Serves: 12
Prep Time: 5 Minutes
Cook Time: 30 Minutes
Total Time: 35 Minutes

INGREDIENTS

- 2 cups oats
- 1 cup blueberries

- 1/3 cup honey
- 1 tsp cinnamon
- 1 ½ tsp vanilla
- 1/3 cup almond butter

DIRECTIONS

1. Mix the honey, vanilla, oats, almond butter, and cinnamon together
2. Fold in the blueberries
3. Refrigerate for at least 30 minutes
4. Form balls from the dough and serve

ZUCCHINI BREAD

Serves: **4**
Prep Time: **10** Minutes
Cook Time: **40** Minutes
Total Time: **50** Minutes

INGREDIENTS

- 4 tbs honey
- 5 tbs oil
- 1 ½ tsp baking soda
- 3 eggs

- ½ cup walnuts
- 2 ½ cups flour
- 4 Medjool dates
- 1 banana
- 2 tsp mixed spice
- 1 ½ cup zucchini

DIRECTIONS

1. Preheat the oven to 350 F
2. Chop the dates and the walnuts
3. Mix the flour, spice and baking soda together
4. Mix the eggs and banana in a food processor then add remaining ingredients and mix
5. Pour the batter into a pan and cook for at least 40 minutes
6. Allow to cool then serve

LUNCH

TOMATO FRITATTA

Serves: **2**
Prep Time: **10** Minutes

Cook Time: **20** Minutes

Total Time: **30** Minutes

INGREDIENTS

- ½ lb. tomato
- **1 tablespoon olive oil**
- ½ **red onion**
- ¼ **tsp salt**

- 2 eggs
- 2 oz. cheddar cheese
- 1 garlic clove
- ¼ tsp dill

DIRECTIONS

1. In a bowl whisk eggs with salt and cheese
2. In a frying pan heat olive oil and pour egg mixture
3. Add remaining ingredients and mix well
4. Serve when ready

YAM ROOT FRITATTA

Serves: 2
Prep Time: 10 Minutes
Cook Time: 20 Minutes
Total Time: 30 Minutes

INGREDIENTS

- ½ cup yam root
- 1 tablespoon olive oil
- ½ red onion
- ¼ tsp salt
- 2 eggs

- 2 oz. cheddar cheese
- 1 garlic clove
- ¼ tsp dill

DIRECTIONS

1. In a bowl whisk eggs with salt and cheese
2. In a frying pan heat olive oil and pour egg mixture
3. Add remaining ingredients and mix well
4. Serve when ready

WATERCRESS FRITATTA

Serves: 2
Prep Time: 10 Minutes
Cook Time: 20 Minutes
Total Time: 30 Minutes

INGREDIENTS

- 1 cup watercress
- 1 tablespoon olive oil
- ½ red onion
- ¼ tsp salt
- 2 eggs
- 2 oz. cheddar cheese

- 1 garlic clove
- ¼ tsp dill

DIRECTIONS

1. In a bowl whisk eggs with salt and cheese
2. In a frying pan heat olive oil and pour egg mixture
3. Add remaining ingredients and mix well
4. Serve when ready

ZUCCHINI FRITATTA

Serves: 2
Prep Time: 10 Minutes
Cook Time: 20 Minutes
Total Time: 30 Minutes

INGREDIENTS

- 1 cup zucchini
- 1 tablespoon olive oil
- ½ red onion
- ¼ tsp salt
- 2 eggs
- 2 oz. parmesan cheese
- 1 garlic clove

- ¼ tsp dill

DIRECTIONS

1. In a skillet sauté zucchini until tender
2. In a bowl whisk eggs with salt and cheese
3. In a frying pan heat olive oil and pour egg mixture
4. Add remaining ingredients and mix well
5. Serve when ready

BROCCOLI FRITATTA

Serves: 2
Prep Time: 10 Minutes
Cook Time: 20 Minutes
Total Time: 30 Minutes

INGREDIENTS

- 1 cup broccoli
- 1 tablespoon olive oil
- ½ red onion
- ¼ tsp salt
- 2 eggs
- 2 oz. cheddar cheese
- 1 garlic clove
- ¼ tsp dill

DIRECTIONS

1. In a skillet sauté broccoli until tender
2. In a bowl whisk eggs with salt and cheese
3. In a frying pan heat olive oil and pour egg mixture
4. Add remaining ingredients and mix well
5. Serve when ready

MOZZARELLA STUFFED CHICKEN BREAST

Serves: 2
Prep Time: 10 Minutes
Cook Time: 25 Minutes
Total Time: 35 Minutes

INGREDIENTS

- 2 chicken breasts
- 1 tsp salt
- 6-7 asparagus spears
- ½ cup mozzarella cheese
- 2 tsp olive oil
- ½ cup bread crumbs

DIRECTIONS

1. Drizzle olive oil and salt over the chicken breast
2. Place the chicken breast in the breadcrumbs bowl and toss well
3. Cut the chicken breast and stuff mozzarella inside
4. Roast chicken breast with asparagus at 400 F for 20-25 minutes
5. When ready remove from the oven and serve

MACARONI AND CHEESE

Serves: 2
Prep Time: 10 Minutes
Cook Time: 20 Minutes
Total Time: 30 Minutes

INGREDIENTS

- 1 cup macaroni
- 1 tablespoon olive oil
- 1 tablespoon all-purpose flour
- 1 tsp salt
- 1 tsp garlic powder
- 1 cup milk
- 1 cup mozzarella cheese
- ½ cup parmesan cheese

DIRECTIONS

1. In a skillet heat olive oil, stir in flour, garlic, salt, milk and cook on low heat
2. Add mozzarella, macaroni and mix well
3. When ready remove from heat and serve with parmesan cheese on top

BUTTERNUT SQUASH BISQUE

Serves: 4
Prep Time: 10 Minutes
Cook Time: 30 Minutes
Total Time: 40 Minutes

INGREDIENTS

- 1 tablespoon olive oil
- ¼ cup red onion
- ½ cup carrots
- 4 cups butternut squash
- 2 cups vegetable stock
- 1 tsp salt

DIRECTIONS

1. In a pot heat olive oil, add onion and cook until tender

2. Add squash and carrots to the pot
3. Add vegetable stock, salt and bring to a boil
4. Simmer on low heat until vegetables are tender
5. Blend the soup until smooth, return to the pot and cook for another 5-10 minutes
6. When ready remove from heat and serve

GARLIC CHICKEN

Serves: 2

Prep Time: **10** Minutes

Cook Time: **40** Minutes

Total Time: **50** Minutes

INGREDIENTS

- 2 tablespoons butter
- 1 tablespoon garlic powder
- 1 tsp rosemary
- 1 tsp salt
- 1 cup honey
- 4 chicken thighs

DIRECTIONS

1. In a saucepan melt butter, add garlic, rosemary, salt and simmer on low heat for 30-60 seconds
2. Add honey and dip the chicken into the mixture
3. Cook for 2-3 minutes, be sure to be well coated
4. Transfer to the oven and bake at 400 F for 30-35 minutes
5. When ready remove from the oven and serve

PASTA WITH CREAM SAUCE

Serves: 2

Prep Time: 10 Minutes

Cook Time: 30 Minutes

Total Time: 40 Minutes

INGREDIENTS

- 2 cups penne pasta
- 2 tablespoons butter
- 1 lb. chicken breast
- 1 tsp garlic
- 1 cup canned pumpkin
- ¼ cup heavy cream
- 1 tablespoon sage leaves
- ¼ tsp salt
- ¼ cup pecans

DIRECTIONS

1. Cook pasta and set aside
2. In a skillet melt butter, add garlic, chicken and cook on medium heat until chicken is cooked
3. Add pasta, pumpkin, heavy cream, sage, salt and pecans
4. Toss to coat and cook on low heat for 5-10 minutes
5. When ready remove from the pot and serve

ROASTED SALAD

Serves: 2

Prep Time: 5 Minutes

Cook Time: 5 Minutes

Total Time: 10 Minutes

INGREDIENTS

- 1 cup cauliflower
- 1 cup broccoli
- 1 cup brussels sprouts
- 1 cup red bell pepper
- 1 cup squash
- 1 tablespoon olive oil

DIRECTIONS

1. In a bowl combine all ingredients together and mix well
2. Serve with dressing

PUMPKIN SALAD

Serves: 2
Prep Time: 5 Minutes
Cook Time: 5 Minutes
Total Time: 10 Minutes

INGREDIENTS

- ½ cauliflower florets
- 1 cup pumpkin
- 1 cup Brussel sprouts
- 1 cup quinoa
- 1 tablespoon olive oil

DIRECTIONS

1. In a bowl combine all ingredients together and mix well
2. Serve with dressing

DUCK SALAD

Serves: 2
Prep Time: 5 Minutes
Cook Time: 5 Minutes
Total Time: 10 Minutes

INGREDIENTS

- 1 cooked duck breast
- ½ lb. Brussel sprouts
- 1 cup broccoli florets
- 1 apple
- 3 oz. blueberries
- 1 tsp olive oil
- 1 cup blueberry salad dressing

DIRECTIONS

1. In a bowl combine all ingredients together and mix well
2. Serve with dressing

BRUSSELS SPROUT SALAD

Serves: **2**

Prep Time: **5** Minutes

Cook Time: **5** Minutes

Total Time: **10** Minutes

INGREDIENTS

- ½ lb. Brussels sprouts
- 1 cup cauliflower florets
- ½ lb. carrot
- 2 oz. lettuce
- 3 oz. cooked breast chicken
- 1 tsp olive oil

DIRECTIONS

1. In a bowl combine all ingredients together and mix well
2. Serve with dressing

ANTI-INFLAMMATORY SALAD

Serves: 2

Prep Time: 5 Minutes

Cook Time: 5 Minutes

Total Time: *10* Minutes

INGREDIENTS

- 1 tablespoon olive oil
- 1 tablespoon apple cider vinegar
- 1 tablespoon lemon juice
- 1 tsp turmeric
- 1 clove garlic
- 1 tsp salt

DIRECTIONS

1. In a bowl combine all ingredients together and mix well
2. Serve with dressing

RED CHICORY SALAD

Serves: 2

Prep Time: 5 Minutes

Cook Time: 5 Minutes

Total Time: 10 Minutes

INGREDIENTS

- 2 red chicory
- 2 fennel bulbs
- ½ cup watercress
- 2 garlic cloves
- 1 tablespoon olive oil

DIRECTIONS

1. In a bowl combine all ingredients together and mix well
2. Serve with dressing

FENNEL SALAD

Serves: **2**

Prep Time: **5** Minutes

Cook Time: **5** Minutes

Total Time: **10** Minutes

INGREDIENTS

- 1 fennel bulb
- 1 tablespoon lemon juice
- ¼ cup olive oil
- 1 tsp mint
- 1 tsp onion

DIRECTIONS

1. In a bowl combine all ingredients together and mix well
2. Serve with dressing

GIGNER CILANTRO SALAD

Serves: 2
Prep Time: 5 Minutes
Cook Time: 5 Minutes
Total Time: 10 Minutes

INGREDIENTS

- 2 lb. sweet potatoes
- ¼ cup olive oil
- 2 tablespoons lemon juice
- ¼ cup scallions
- ¼ cup cilantro
- ¼ tsp salt

DIRECTIONS

1. In a bowl combine all ingredients together and mix well
2. Serve with dressing

DINNER

CHEESE MACARONI

Serves: **1**

Prep Time: **10** Minutes

Cook Time: **20** Minutes

Total Time: **30** Minutes

INGREDIENTS

- 1 lb. macaroni
- 1 cup cheddar cheese
- 1 cup Monterey Jack cheese
- 1 cup mozzarella cheese
- ¼ tsp salt
- ¼ tsp pepper

DIRECTIONS

1. In a pot bring water to a boil
2. Add pasta and cook until al dente
3. In a bowl combine all cheese together and add it to the pasta
4. When ready transfer to a bowl, add salt, pepper and serve

POTATO CASSEROLE

Serves: 2

Prep Time: *10*   Minutes

Cook Time: *20*   Minutes

Total Time: *30*   Minutes

INGREDIENTS

- 5-6 large potatoes
- ¼ cup sour cream
- ½ cup butter
- 5-6 bacon strips
- 1-2 cups mozzarella cheese
- ¼ cup heavy cream

DIRECTIONS

1. Place the potatoes in a pot with boiling water, cook until tender
2. Place the potatoes in a bowl, add sour cream, butter, cheese and mix well
3. In a baking dish place the bacon strips and cover with potato mixture
4. Add remaining mozzarella cheese on top
5. Bake at 325 F for 15-18 minutes or until the mozzarella is fully melted
6. When ready remove from the oven and serve

CHEESE STUFFED SHELLS

Serves: 2

Prep Time: **10** Minutes

Cook Time: **30** Minutes

Total Time: **40** Minutes

INGREDIENTS

- 2-3 cups macaroni
- 2 cups cream cheese
- 1 cup spaghetti sauce
- 1 cup onions
- 1 cup mozzarella cheese

DIRECTIONS

1. In a pot boil water and add shells
2. Cook for 12-15 minutes
3. In a baking dish add spaghetti sauce
4. In a bowl combine cream cheese, onion and set aside
5. Add cream cheese to the shells and place them into the baking dish
6. Bake at 325 F for 30 minutes or until golden brown
7. When ready remove from the oven and serve

POTATO SOUP

Serves: **4-6**

Prep Time: **10** Minutes

Cook Time: **50** Minutes

Total Time: **60** Minutes

INGREDIENTS

- 1 onion
- 2-3 carrots
- 2 tablespoons flour
- 5-6 large potatoes
- 2 cups milk
- 2 cups bouillon
- 1 cup water
- 2 cups milk
- 1 tsp salt
- 1 tsp pepper

DIRECTIONS

1. In a saucepan melt butter and sauce carrots, garlic and onion for 4-5 minutes
2. Add flour, milk, potatoes, bouillon and cook for another 15-20 minutes

3. Add pepper and remaining ingredients and cook on low heat for 20-30 minutes
4. When ready remove from heat and serve

CHICKEN ALFREDO

Serves: 2

Prep Time: 10 Minutes

Cook Time: 20 Minutes

Total Time: 30 Minutes

INGREDIENTS

- 2-3 chicken breasts
- 1 lb. rotini
- 1 cup parmesan cheese
- 1 cup olive oil
- 1 tsp salt
- 1 tsp black pepper
- 1 tsp parsley

DIRECTIONS

1. In a pot add the rotini and cook on low heat for 12-15 minutes
2. In a frying pan heat olive oil, add chicken, salt, parsley, and cook until the chicken is brown
3. Drain the rotini and place the rotini in pan with chicken
4. Cook for 2-3 minutes

5. When ready remove from heat and serve with parmesan cheese on top

BUTTERNUT SQUASH PIZZA

Serves: **4-6**

Prep Time: **10** Minutes

Cook Time: **15** Minutes

Total Time: **25** Minutes

INGREDIENTS

- 2 cups butternut squash
- ¼ tsp salt
- 1 pizza crust
- 5-6 tablespoons alfredo sauce
- 1 tsp olive oil
- 4-5 cups baby spinach
- 2-3 oz. goat cheese

DIRECTIONS

1. Place the pizza crust on a baking dish and spread the alfredo sauce
2. In a skillet sauté spinach and place it over the pizza crust
3. Add goat cheese, butternut squash, olive oil and salt
4. Bake pizza at 425 F for 8-10 minutes
5. When ready remove from the oven and serve

PENNE WITH ASPARAGUS

Serves: 2

Prep Time: **10** Minutes

Cook Time: **20** Minutes

Total Time: **30** Minutes

INGREDIENTS

- 6-7 oz. penne pasta
- 2-3 bacon slices
- ¼ cup red onion
- 2 cups asparagus
- 1 cup chicken broth
- 2-3 cups spinach leaves
- ¼ cup parmesan cheese

DIRECTIONS

1. Cook pasta until al dente
2. In a skillet cook bacon until crispy and set aside
3. In a pan add onion, asparagus, broth and cook on low heat for 5-10 minutes
4. Add spinach, cheese, pepper, pasta and cook for another 5-6 minutes
5. When ready sprinkle bacon and serve

NOODLE SOUP

Serves: **4**

Prep Time: **10** Minutes

Cook Time: **20** Minutes

Total Time: **30** Minutes

INGREDIENTS

- 2-3 cups water
- 1 can chicken broth
- 1 tablespoon olive oil
- ¼ red onion
- ¼ cup celery
- ¼ tsp salt
- ¼ tsp black pepper
- 5-6 oz. fusilli pasta
- 2 cups chicken breast
- 2 tablespoons parsley

DIRECTIONS

1. In a pot boil water with broth
2. In a saucepan heat oil, add carrot, pepper, celery, onion, salt and sauté until tender
3. Add broth mixture to the mixture and pasta

4. Cook until al dente and stir in chicken breast, cook until chicken breast is tender
5. When ready remove from heat, stir in parsley and serve

TOMATO WRAP

Serves: **4**

Prep Time: **5** Minutes

Cook Time: **15** Minutes

Total Time: **20** Minutes

INGREDIENTS

- 1 cup corn
- 1 cup tomatoes
- 1 cup pickles
- 1 tablespoon olive oil
- 1 tablespoon mayonnaise
- 6-7 turkey slices
- 2-3 whole-wheat tortillas
- 1 cup romaine lettuce

DIRECTIONS

1. In a bowl combine tomatoes, pickles, olive oil, corn and set aside
2. Place the turkey slices over the tortillas and top with tomato mixture and mayonnaise
3. Roll and serve

THYME COD

Serves: 2
Prep Time: 5 Minutes
Cook Time: 15 Minutes
Total Time: 20 Minutes

INGREDIENTS

- 1 tablespoon olive oil
- ½ red onion
- 1 can tomatoes
- 2-3 springs thyme
- 2-3 cod fillets

DIRECTIONS

1. In a frying pan heat olive oil and sauté onion, stir in tomatoes, spring thyme and cook for 5-6 minutes
2. Add cod fillets, cover and cook for 5-6 minutes per side
3. When ready remove from heat and serve

VEGGIE STIR-FRY

Serves: 2

Prep Time: 10   Minutes

Cook Time: 20   Minutes

Total Time: 30   Minutes

INGREDIENTS

- 1 tablespoon cornstarch
- 1 garlic clove
- ¼ cup olive oil
- ¼ head broccoli
- ¼ cup show peas
- ½ cup carrots
- ¼ cup green beans
- 1 tablespoon soy sauce
- ½ cup onion

DIRECTIONS

1. In a bowl combine garlic, olive oil, cornstarch and mix well
2. Add the rest of the ingredients and toss to coat
3. In a skillet cook vegetables mixture until tender
4. When ready transfer to a plate garnish with ginger and serve

SMOOTHIES

PROBIOTIC SMOOTHIE

Serves: 1
Prep Time: 5 Minutes
Cook Time: 5 Minutes
Total Time: 10 Minutes

INGREDIENTS

- 1 pear
- ¼ cup almond milk
- 1 cup Greek yogurt
- 1 tsp cinnamon
- 1 cup ice

DIRECTIONS

1. In a blender place all ingredients and blend until smooth
2. Pour smoothie in a glass and serve

ENERGY BOOSTING SMOOTHIE

Serves: **1**

Prep Time: **5** Minutes

Cook Time: **5** Minutes

Total Time: **10** Minutes

INGREDIENTS

- 1 banana
- 1 pear
- 1 avocado
- 1 cup spinach
- 1 cup ice

DIRECTIONS

1. In a blender place all ingredients and blend until smooth
2. Pour smoothie in a glass and serve

BLUEBERRY SMOOTHIE

Serves: **1**

Prep Time: **5** Minutes

Cook Time: **5** Minutes

Total Time: **10** Minutes

INGREDIENTS

- 1 cup almond milk
- ¼ cup Greek yogurt
- ¼ tsp vanilla extract
- 1 tsp honey
- 1 cup kale
- ¼ cup baby spinach
- 1 cup blueberries

DIRECTIONS

1. In a blender place all ingredients and blend until smooth
2. Pour smoothie in a glass and serve

RED CAPSICUM JUICE

Serves: **1**

Prep Time: **5** Minutes

Cook Time: **5** Minutes

Total Time: **10** Minutes

INGREDIENTS

- 1 cup red capsicum
- 1 cup carrot
- 1 cup apple
- 1 cup ice

DIRECTIONS

1. In a blender place all ingredients and blend until smooth
2. Pour smoothie in a glass and serve

GREEN SMOOTHIE

Serves: 1

Prep Time: 5 Minutes

Cook Time: 5 Minutes

Total Time: 10 Minutes

INGREDIENTS

- 1 tablespoon tyrosine
- ½ cup kale
- ½ cup watercress
- ¼ cup spinach
- ¼ cup antioxidants
- 1 cup ice

DIRECTIONS

1. In a blender place all ingredients and blend until smooth
2. Pour smoothie in a glass and serve

RASPBERRY MOJITO FRAPPE

Serves: **1**

Prep Time: **5** Minutes

Cook Time: **5** Minutes

Total Time: **10** Minutes

INGREDIENTS

- 1 cup raspberries
- 4-5 mint leaves
- 1 tsp maple syrup
- 1 cup ice

DIRECTIONS

1. **In a blender place all ingredients and blend until smooth**
2. **Pour smoothie in a glass and serve**

MANGO SMOOTHIE

Serves: 1
Prep Time: 5 Minutes
Cook Time: 5 Minutes
Total Time: 10 Minutes

INGREDIENTS

- 1 cup milk
- 1 passionfruit
- 1 banana
- 1 mango
- 1 tsp chia seeds

DIRECTIONS

1. Blend the ingredients together except the passion fruit
2. Serve topped with passionfruit seeds

PINEAPPLE SMOOTHIE

Serves: **1**

Prep Time: **5** Minutes

Cook Time: **5** Minutes

Total Time: **10** Minutes

INGREDIENTS

- 1 cup apricot nectar
- 1 banana
- ½ mango
- Pineapple

DIRECTIONS

1. Mix everything together until smooth
2. Serve immediately

BLUEBERRIES SMOOTHIE

Serves: **1**

Prep Time: **5** Minutes

Cook Time: **5** Minutes

Total Time: **10** Minutes

INGREDIENTS

- 1 banana
- Blueberries
- Milk
- 1 mango

DIRECTIONS

1. Blend everything together until smooth
2. Serve immediately

PEANUT BUTTER & BANANA SMOOTHIE

Serves: **1**

Prep Time: **5** Minutes

Cook Time: **5** Minutes

Total Time: **10** Minutes

INGREDIENTS

- 1 banana
- 1 cup coconut milk
- ¼ cup peanut butter
- 1 tablespoon honey
- 1 cup ice

DIRECTIONS

1. In a blender place all ingredients and blend until smooth
2. Pour smoothie in a glass and serve

GROOVY SMOOTHIE

Serves: **1**

Prep Time: **5** Minutes

Cook Time: **5** Minutes

Total Time: **10** Minutes

INGREDIENTS

- 1 banana
- 1 cup grapes
- ¼ cup Greek yogurt
- ¼ apple
- 1 cup baby spinach

DIRECTIONS

1. In a blender place all ingredients and blend until smooth
2. Pour smoothie in a glass and serve

THANK YOU FOR READING THIS BOOK!

CPSIA information can be obtained
at www.ICGtesting.com
Printed in the USA
LVHW032212210321
682038LV00007B/162